50 Holiday Feasts: Recipes for Special Occasions

By: Kelly Johnson

Table of Contents

- Roasted Turkey with Herb Butter
- Honey-Glazed Ham
- Beef Wellington
- Garlic Mashed Potatoes
- Classic Stuffing with Sausage
- Gravy from Scratch
- Baked Mac and Cheese
- Cranberry Sauce with Orange
- Roasted Brussels Sprouts with Balsamic Glaze
- Pumpkin Pie
- Pecan Pie
- Apple Crisp
- Yorkshire Pudding
- Baked Ziti with Ricotta
- Sweet Potato Casserole
- Green Bean Almondine
- Garlic Roasted Mushrooms
- Beef Rib Roast
- Lemon Herb Roast Chicken
- Stuffed Acorn Squash
- Caesar Salad with Homemade Dressing
- Roasted Carrots with Honey and Thyme
- Buttermilk Biscuits
- Spinach and Artichoke Dip
- Shrimp Cocktail
- Lobster Newberg
- Chicken and Dumplings
- Cranberry Orange Bread
- Cornbread Dressing
- Eggnog Cheesecake
- Chocolate Yule Log
- Roasted Leg of Lamb
- Maple-Glazed Carrots
- Roasted Beet Salad with Goat Cheese
- Fennel and Orange Salad

- Mulled Wine
- Hot Chocolate Bar
- Gingerbread Cookies
- Pomegranate and Feta Salad
- Bourbon-Pecan Cake
- Cinnamon Rolls
- Spiced Apple Cider
- Fig and Prosciutto Salad
- Braised Short Ribs
- Mincemeat Pie
- Ratatouille
- Roasted Potatoes with Rosemary
- Trifle with Berries and Custard
- Vanilla and Almond Panettone
- Chocolate Mint Tart

Roasted Turkey with Herb Butter

Ingredients:

- 1 whole turkey (10-12 lbs)
- 1/2 cup unsalted butter, softened
- 2 tbsp fresh thyme, chopped
- 2 tbsp fresh rosemary, chopped
- 2 tbsp fresh sage, chopped
- 1 lemon, quartered
- 4 cloves garlic, smashed
- 1 onion, quartered
- Salt and pepper to taste

Instructions:

1. Preheat the oven to 325°F (165°C).
2. In a small bowl, mix the softened butter with the herbs, salt, and pepper.
3. Pat the turkey dry with paper towels. Carefully lift the skin and rub the herb butter underneath the skin and all over the turkey.
4. Stuff the cavity with lemon, garlic, and onion.
5. Place the turkey on a rack in a roasting pan. Tuck the wings under the turkey and season the outside with salt and pepper.
6. Roast the turkey for about 13-15 minutes per pound, basting occasionally with the pan juices. The internal temperature should reach 165°F (74°C).
7. Let the turkey rest for 20-30 minutes before carving.

Honey-Glazed Ham

Ingredients:

- 1 bone-in ham (8-10 lbs)
- 1/2 cup honey
- 1/4 cup Dijon mustard
- 1/4 cup brown sugar
- 1/4 cup apple cider vinegar
- 1/4 cup orange juice
- 1 tsp ground cloves

Instructions:

1. Preheat the oven to 325°F (165°C).
2. Score the top of the ham in a diamond pattern and place it in a roasting pan.
3. In a small saucepan, combine honey, mustard, brown sugar, vinegar, orange juice, and cloves. Simmer over medium heat for 5-10 minutes until the glaze thickens.
4. Brush the ham with the glaze, reserving some for later.
5. Roast the ham for 1 1/2 to 2 hours, basting every 20 minutes with the glaze. The ham is done when the internal temperature reaches 140°F (60°C).
6. Let the ham rest before slicing and serving.

Beef Wellington

Ingredients:

- 2 lb beef tenderloin, trimmed
- 2 tbsp olive oil
- Salt and pepper to taste
- 2 tbsp Dijon mustard
- 8 oz cremini or white mushrooms, finely chopped
- 1/4 cup shallots, minced
- 2 tbsp unsalted butter
- 1/2 cup prosciutto, thinly sliced
- 1 sheet puff pastry, thawed
- 1 egg, beaten (for egg wash)

Instructions:

1. Preheat the oven to 400°F (200°C).
2. Season the beef tenderloin with salt and pepper. Heat olive oil in a skillet and sear the beef on all sides until browned. Remove from heat and brush with Dijon mustard. Let cool.
3. In the same skillet, melt butter and sauté shallots and mushrooms until the mushrooms release their moisture and become dry. Let cool.
4. Lay prosciutto on plastic wrap, spread the mushroom mixture over it, and roll the beef tightly in the prosciutto. Wrap in puff pastry and seal the edges.
5. Brush the pastry with egg wash and place the Wellington on a baking sheet.
6. Bake for 35-40 minutes, or until the pastry is golden and the internal temperature reaches 125°F (52°C) for medium-rare.
7. Let the Wellington rest for 10-15 minutes before slicing.

Garlic Mashed Potatoes

Ingredients:

- 2 lbs Yukon Gold potatoes, peeled and cubed
- 4 cloves garlic, peeled
- 1/2 cup unsalted butter
- 1 cup whole milk
- Salt and pepper to taste
- Chives, chopped (for garnish)

Instructions:

1. In a large pot, boil the potatoes and garlic cloves in salted water for 15-20 minutes until tender.
2. Drain the potatoes and garlic, then return them to the pot.
3. Mash the potatoes and garlic together until smooth. Add butter and milk, and continue mashing until creamy.
4. Season with salt and pepper, and garnish with chopped chives.

Classic Stuffing with Sausage

Ingredients:

- 1 lb Italian sausage, casings removed
- 1 onion, chopped
- 2 celery stalks, chopped
- 2 cups chicken broth
- 10 cups cubed day-old bread
- 1/4 cup fresh parsley, chopped
- 1 tbsp fresh sage, chopped
- 1 tsp dried thyme
- Salt and pepper to taste

Instructions:

1. Preheat the oven to 350°F (175°C).
2. In a large skillet, cook the sausage until browned, breaking it up with a spoon. Remove and set aside.
3. In the same skillet, sauté the onion and celery until softened.
4. In a large bowl, combine the bread cubes, sausage, onion, celery, herbs, and chicken broth. Mix well and season with salt and pepper.
5. Transfer the mixture to a greased baking dish and cover with foil.
6. Bake for 30-40 minutes, then remove the foil and bake for an additional 10 minutes until golden and crispy on top.

Gravy from Scratch

Ingredients:

- 1/4 cup unsalted butter
- 1/4 cup all-purpose flour
- 2 cups turkey or chicken broth
- 1/2 cup pan drippings from roasted turkey
- Salt and pepper to taste

Instructions:

1. In a saucepan, melt butter over medium heat. Stir in flour and cook for 1-2 minutes until it forms a roux.
2. Gradually whisk in the broth and pan drippings, and bring to a simmer.
3. Cook for 5-7 minutes until the gravy thickens. Season with salt and pepper.
4. Strain the gravy and serve with turkey.

Baked Mac and Cheese

Ingredients:

- 1 lb elbow macaroni
- 2 cups shredded sharp cheddar cheese
- 1 cup shredded mozzarella cheese
- 1/4 cup grated Parmesan cheese
- 1/4 cup unsalted butter
- 2 cups whole milk
- 1/4 cup all-purpose flour
- 1/2 tsp garlic powder
- Salt and pepper to taste
- 1/2 cup breadcrumbs (for topping)

Instructions:

1. Preheat the oven to 350°F (175°C).
2. Cook the macaroni according to package instructions, then drain and set aside.
3. In a saucepan, melt butter over medium heat. Stir in flour and cook for 1-2 minutes.
4. Gradually whisk in milk, and cook until the sauce thickens.
5. Stir in the cheeses, garlic powder, salt, and pepper. Mix until the cheese is melted and smooth.
6. Combine the cooked macaroni and cheese sauce in a large bowl, then transfer to a greased baking dish.
7. Top with breadcrumbs and bake for 25-30 minutes until bubbly and golden.

Cranberry Sauce with Orange

Ingredients:

- 12 oz fresh cranberries
- 1 cup sugar
- 1/2 cup orange juice
- Zest of 1 orange
- 1/4 tsp ground cinnamon

Instructions:

1. In a saucepan, combine cranberries, sugar, orange juice, and cinnamon.
2. Bring to a boil, then reduce the heat and simmer for 10-15 minutes, stirring occasionally.
3. Once the cranberries burst and the sauce thickens, remove from heat.
4. Stir in the orange zest and let cool before serving.

Roasted Brussels Sprouts with Balsamic Glaze

Ingredients:

- 1 lb Brussels sprouts, trimmed and halved
- 2 tbsp olive oil
- Salt and pepper to taste
- 2 tbsp balsamic vinegar
- 1 tbsp honey
- 1 tbsp Dijon mustard

Instructions:

1. Preheat the oven to 400°F (200°C).
2. Toss the Brussels sprouts with olive oil, salt, and pepper. Arrange them in a single layer on a baking sheet.
3. Roast for 20-25 minutes, flipping halfway through, until the sprouts are golden and crispy on the edges.
4. While the sprouts are roasting, whisk together balsamic vinegar, honey, and Dijon mustard in a small saucepan over medium heat. Simmer for 3-5 minutes until the glaze thickens.
5. Drizzle the balsamic glaze over the roasted Brussels sprouts before serving.

Pumpkin Pie

Ingredients:

- 1 (15 oz) can pumpkin puree
- 3/4 cup granulated sugar
- 1 tsp ground cinnamon
- 1/2 tsp ground ginger
- 1/4 tsp ground nutmeg
- 1/4 tsp salt
- 2 large eggs
- 1 1/2 cups heavy cream
- 1 tsp vanilla extract
- 1 pre-made pie crust

Instructions:

1. Preheat the oven to 425°F (220°C).
2. In a large bowl, whisk together pumpkin puree, sugar, cinnamon, ginger, nutmeg, and salt.
3. Beat in the eggs, followed by the heavy cream and vanilla extract.
4. Pour the mixture into the pie crust and smooth the top.
5. Bake for 15 minutes, then reduce the oven temperature to 350°F (175°C) and bake for an additional 40-45 minutes, or until the filling is set and a toothpick inserted comes out clean.
6. Let the pie cool before serving.

Pecan Pie

Ingredients:

- 1 pie crust, unbaked
- 1 1/2 cups pecans, chopped
- 1 cup corn syrup
- 3/4 cup brown sugar
- 1/4 cup unsalted butter, melted
- 3 large eggs
- 1 tsp vanilla extract
- 1/4 tsp salt

Instructions:

1. Preheat the oven to 350°F (175°C).
2. In a medium bowl, whisk together corn syrup, brown sugar, melted butter, eggs, vanilla extract, and salt.
3. Stir in the chopped pecans and pour the mixture into the unbaked pie crust.
4. Bake for 50-60 minutes, or until the filling is set and the top is golden brown.
5. Let the pie cool before serving.

Apple Crisp

Ingredients:

- 6 cups apples, peeled, cored, and sliced
- 1 tbsp lemon juice
- 1/2 cup granulated sugar
- 1 tsp ground cinnamon
- 1/4 tsp ground nutmeg
- 1/4 tsp salt
- 1/2 cup old-fashioned rolled oats
- 1/2 cup all-purpose flour
- 1/2 cup packed brown sugar
- 1/4 cup unsalted butter, cubed

Instructions:

1. Preheat the oven to 350°F (175°C).
2. In a large bowl, toss the sliced apples with lemon juice, granulated sugar, cinnamon, nutmeg, and salt. Transfer to a greased 9x13-inch baking dish.
3. In another bowl, combine oats, flour, brown sugar, and butter. Use a pastry cutter or your hands to work the butter into the dry ingredients until crumbly.
4. Sprinkle the oat mixture evenly over the apples.
5. Bake for 40-45 minutes, or until the topping is golden brown and the apples are tender.

Yorkshire Pudding

Ingredients:

- 1 cup all-purpose flour
- 1/2 tsp salt
- 1 cup whole milk
- 2 large eggs
- 1/4 cup vegetable oil

Instructions:

1. Preheat the oven to 425°F (220°C).
2. In a medium bowl, whisk together flour and salt. Add milk and eggs, and whisk until smooth.
3. Pour the oil into a 12-cup muffin tin, filling each cup with about 1 tsp of oil. Place the tin in the oven to heat the oil for 10 minutes.
4. Carefully pour the batter into the hot muffin cups, filling each about halfway.
5. Bake for 20-25 minutes, or until the Yorkshire puddings have risen and are golden brown.
6. Serve immediately.

Baked Ziti with Ricotta

Ingredients:

- 1 lb ziti pasta
- 2 cups marinara sauce
- 1 cup ricotta cheese
- 1 1/2 cups shredded mozzarella cheese
- 1/4 cup grated Parmesan cheese
- 1/4 cup fresh basil, chopped
- Salt and pepper to taste

Instructions:

1. Preheat the oven to 375°F (190°C).
2. Cook the ziti according to the package directions. Drain and set aside.
3. In a large bowl, mix together the marinara sauce, ricotta cheese, mozzarella, Parmesan, and fresh basil. Season with salt and pepper.
4. Add the cooked ziti to the sauce mixture and stir to combine.
5. Transfer to a greased 9x13-inch baking dish and top with additional mozzarella and Parmesan cheese.
6. Bake for 25-30 minutes, or until the cheese is melted and bubbly.
7. Let the baked ziti rest for a few minutes before serving.

Sweet Potato Casserole

Ingredients:

- 4 large sweet potatoes, peeled and cubed
- 1/4 cup unsalted butter
- 1/4 cup brown sugar
- 1 tsp ground cinnamon
- 1/2 tsp ground nutmeg
- 1/2 tsp vanilla extract
- 1/4 tsp salt
- 1/2 cup mini marshmallows (optional)

Instructions:

1. Preheat the oven to 350°F (175°C).
2. Boil the sweet potatoes in salted water for 15-20 minutes until tender. Drain and mash the potatoes.
3. Stir in the butter, brown sugar, cinnamon, nutmeg, vanilla extract, and salt until smooth.
4. Transfer the mixture to a greased baking dish and top with marshmallows, if using.
5. Bake for 20-25 minutes, or until the marshmallows are golden brown.
6. Serve warm.

Green Bean Almondine

Ingredients:

- 1 lb green beans, trimmed
- 1/4 cup unsalted butter
- 1/4 cup sliced almonds
- 1 clove garlic, minced
- 1 tbsp lemon juice
- Salt and pepper to taste

Instructions:

1. Bring a large pot of salted water to a boil. Add the green beans and cook for 5-7 minutes until tender-crisp. Drain and set aside.
2. In a large skillet, melt the butter over medium heat. Add the almonds and cook for 2-3 minutes, stirring occasionally, until golden.
3. Add the garlic to the skillet and cook for another 1-2 minutes.
4. Stir in the cooked green beans and lemon juice, and season with salt and pepper.
5. Serve immediately.

Garlic Roasted Mushrooms

Ingredients:

- 1 lb button mushrooms, cleaned and halved
- 4 cloves garlic, minced
- 2 tbsp olive oil
- 1 tbsp fresh thyme, chopped
- Salt and pepper to taste
- 1 tbsp balsamic vinegar (optional)

Instructions:

1. Preheat the oven to 400°F (200°C).
2. Toss the mushrooms with olive oil, garlic, thyme, salt, and pepper in a large bowl.
3. Spread the mushrooms in a single layer on a baking sheet.
4. Roast for 20-25 minutes, stirring halfway through, until the mushrooms are golden brown and tender.
5. Drizzle with balsamic vinegar before serving (optional).

Beef Rib Roast

Ingredients:

- 5-6 lb beef rib roast (bone-in)
- 2 tbsp olive oil
- 3 cloves garlic, minced
- 2 tbsp fresh rosemary, chopped
- 1 tbsp fresh thyme, chopped
- Salt and pepper to taste

Instructions:

1. Preheat the oven to 450°F (230°C).
2. Rub the beef rib roast with olive oil, garlic, rosemary, thyme, salt, and pepper.
3. Place the roast on a rack in a roasting pan and roast for 15 minutes at 450°F.
4. Reduce the oven temperature to 350°F (175°C) and continue roasting for about 1.5 to 2 hours for medium-rare (internal temperature should be 125°F).
5. Let the roast rest for 10-15 minutes before slicing and serving.

Lemon Herb Roast Chicken

Ingredients:

- 1 whole chicken (3-4 lbs)
- 2 tbsp olive oil
- 1 lemon, halved
- 4 cloves garlic, smashed
- 1 tbsp fresh thyme, chopped
- 1 tbsp fresh rosemary, chopped
- Salt and pepper to taste

Instructions:

1. Preheat the oven to 425°F (220°C).
2. Rub the chicken with olive oil, salt, and pepper. Stuff the cavity with lemon halves, garlic, thyme, and rosemary.
3. Place the chicken on a roasting pan and roast for 1 hour and 20 minutes, or until the internal temperature reaches 165°F (75°C) and the skin is golden brown.
4. Let the chicken rest for 10 minutes before carving.

Stuffed Acorn Squash

Ingredients:

- 2 acorn squashes, halved and seeds removed
- 2 tbsp olive oil
- Salt and pepper to taste
- 1/2 cup quinoa, cooked
- 1/2 cup cranberries, dried
- 1/4 cup pecans, chopped
- 2 tbsp maple syrup
- 1 tbsp fresh parsley, chopped

Instructions:

1. Preheat the oven to 375°F (190°C).
2. Brush the cut sides of the squash with olive oil and season with salt and pepper.
3. Place the squash halves cut-side down on a baking sheet and roast for 40-45 minutes, or until tender.
4. Meanwhile, prepare the quinoa according to package instructions. Stir in cranberries, pecans, maple syrup, and parsley.
5. Stuff the roasted squash halves with the quinoa mixture and serve warm.

Caesar Salad with Homemade Dressing

Ingredients:

- 1 large head romaine lettuce, chopped
- 1/2 cup homemade Caesar dressing (see below)
- 1/4 cup Parmesan cheese, grated
- Croutons (optional)

For Caesar Dressing:

- 1 egg yolk
- 2 tbsp Dijon mustard
- 2 cloves garlic, minced
- 2 tbsp lemon juice
- 1 tsp Worcestershire sauce
- 1/2 cup olive oil
- 1/4 cup grated Parmesan cheese
- Salt and pepper to taste

Instructions:

1. For the dressing: whisk together egg yolk, Dijon mustard, garlic, lemon juice, and Worcestershire sauce in a bowl.
2. Gradually whisk in olive oil until the mixture thickens.
3. Stir in Parmesan cheese and season with salt and pepper.
4. Toss the chopped lettuce with the dressing, then sprinkle with additional Parmesan and croutons, if desired.

Roasted Carrots with Honey and Thyme

Ingredients:

- 1 lb carrots, peeled and cut into sticks
- 2 tbsp olive oil
- 1 tbsp honey
- 1 tbsp fresh thyme, chopped
- Salt and pepper to taste

Instructions:

1. Preheat the oven to 400°F (200°C).
2. Toss the carrots with olive oil, honey, thyme, salt, and pepper.
3. Spread the carrots in a single layer on a baking sheet.
4. Roast for 20-25 minutes, or until the carrots are tender and lightly caramelized, stirring halfway through.

Buttermilk Biscuits

Ingredients:

- 2 cups all-purpose flour
- 2 tsp baking powder
- 1/2 tsp baking soda
- 1/2 tsp salt
- 1/4 cup unsalted butter, cold and cubed
- 3/4 cup buttermilk

Instructions:

1. Preheat the oven to 450°F (230°C).
2. In a large bowl, whisk together flour, baking powder, baking soda, and salt.
3. Cut in the cold butter until the mixture resembles coarse crumbs.
4. Stir in the buttermilk until the dough comes together.
5. Turn the dough onto a floured surface and gently knead 4-5 times. Pat the dough into a 1-inch thick rectangle.
6. Use a biscuit cutter to cut out biscuits and place them on a baking sheet.
7. Bake for 10-12 minutes, or until golden brown.

Spinach and Artichoke Dip

Ingredients:

- 1 (10 oz) package frozen spinach, thawed and drained
- 1 (14 oz) can artichoke hearts, drained and chopped
- 1 cup cream cheese, softened
- 1/2 cup sour cream
- 1/2 cup mayonnaise
- 1 cup Parmesan cheese, grated
- 1 cup mozzarella cheese, shredded
- 2 cloves garlic, minced
- Salt and pepper to taste

Instructions:

1. Preheat the oven to 375°F (190°C).
2. In a large bowl, combine spinach, artichokes, cream cheese, sour cream, mayonnaise, Parmesan, mozzarella, and garlic.
3. Season with salt and pepper and stir until smooth.
4. Transfer the mixture to a greased baking dish and bake for 25-30 minutes, or until bubbly and golden on top.
5. Serve warm with chips or sliced baguette.

Shrimp Cocktail

Ingredients:

- 1 lb large shrimp, peeled and deveined
- 1 lemon, sliced
- 2 cloves garlic, smashed
- 1 tbsp Old Bay seasoning
- 1/4 cup cocktail sauce
- Fresh parsley for garnish

Instructions:

1. Bring a large pot of salted water to a boil. Add the shrimp, lemon slices, garlic, and Old Bay seasoning.
2. Cook the shrimp for 2-3 minutes until pink and opaque.
3. Drain the shrimp and transfer to an ice bath to cool.
4. Serve chilled with cocktail sauce and garnish with fresh parsley.

Lobster Newberg

Ingredients:

- 2 lobster tails, cooked and chopped
- 1/2 cup heavy cream
- 2 tbsp butter
- 4 large egg yolks
- 1 tbsp brandy (optional)
- 1 tbsp lemon juice
- Salt and pepper to taste
- Fresh parsley for garnish

Instructions:

1. In a saucepan, melt butter over medium heat. Add heavy cream and bring to a simmer.
2. Whisk in egg yolks and cook until the sauce thickens, about 3-4 minutes.
3. Stir in brandy (if using), lemon juice, salt, and pepper.
4. Add the chopped lobster meat and stir until heated through.
5. Serve in individual ramekins or lobster shells, garnished with fresh parsley.

Chicken and Dumplings

Ingredients:

- 1 lb chicken breasts, cooked and shredded
- 1 onion, diced
- 2 carrots, chopped
- 2 celery stalks, chopped
- 4 cups chicken broth
- 2 cups milk
- 2 tbsp butter
- 1 tsp thyme
- Salt and pepper to taste

For Dumplings:

- 1 cup all-purpose flour
- 1 tsp baking powder
- 1/4 tsp salt
- 1/2 cup milk
- 2 tbsp butter, melted

Instructions:

1. In a large pot, melt butter over medium heat. Add onions, carrots, and celery, and cook until softened, about 5 minutes.
2. Add chicken broth, milk, shredded chicken, thyme, salt, and pepper. Bring to a simmer.
3. For the dumplings, mix together flour, baking powder, salt, milk, and melted butter to form a dough.
4. Drop spoonfuls of dumpling dough into the simmering soup. Cover and cook for 15-20 minutes, or until dumplings are cooked through.
5. Serve hot with a sprinkle of fresh parsley.

Cranberry Orange Bread

Ingredients:

- 2 cups all-purpose flour
- 1 cup sugar
- 1 tsp baking powder
- 1/2 tsp baking soda
- 1/2 tsp salt
- 1 cup fresh cranberries, chopped
- 1/2 cup orange juice
- 1/4 cup vegetable oil
- 1 large egg
- Zest of 1 orange

Instructions:

1. Preheat the oven to 350°F (175°C). Grease and flour a loaf pan.
2. In a large bowl, combine flour, sugar, baking powder, baking soda, and salt.
3. In a separate bowl, whisk together orange juice, vegetable oil, egg, and orange zest.
4. Add wet ingredients to dry ingredients and stir until just combined. Gently fold in chopped cranberries.
5. Pour the batter into the prepared loaf pan and bake for 60-70 minutes, or until a toothpick comes out clean.

Cornbread Dressing

Ingredients:

- 1 batch cornbread, crumbled (see below)
- 1 onion, chopped
- 2 celery stalks, chopped
- 2 tbsp butter
- 2 cups chicken broth
- 1 tsp sage
- Salt and pepper to taste
- 1 egg, beaten

For Cornbread:

- 1 cup cornmeal
- 1 cup flour
- 1 tbsp baking powder
- 1/2 tsp salt
- 1 cup milk
- 1/4 cup butter, melted
- 1 egg

Instructions:

1. For the cornbread: Preheat the oven to 425°F (220°C). Grease a baking dish.
2. In a bowl, mix cornmeal, flour, baking powder, salt, milk, butter, and egg. Pour the batter into the baking dish and bake for 20-25 minutes, or until golden brown.
3. For the dressing: In a pan, sauté onion and celery in butter until softened, about 5 minutes.
4. In a large bowl, combine crumbled cornbread, sautéed vegetables, chicken broth, sage, salt, pepper, and beaten egg.
5. Transfer the mixture to a greased baking dish and bake at 350°F (175°C) for 25-30 minutes, or until the top is golden.

Eggnog Cheesecake

Ingredients:

- 1 1/2 cups graham cracker crumbs
- 1/4 cup sugar
- 1/2 cup butter, melted
- 3 (8 oz) packages cream cheese, softened
- 1 cup sugar
- 3 eggs
- 1/2 cup eggnog
- 1/2 tsp nutmeg
- 1 tsp vanilla extract

Instructions:

1. Preheat the oven to 325°F (165°C).
2. Mix graham cracker crumbs, sugar, and melted butter in a bowl. Press into the bottom of a springform pan.
3. In a large bowl, beat cream cheese and sugar until smooth. Add eggs one at a time, beating after each addition.
4. Stir in eggnog, nutmeg, and vanilla extract.
5. Pour the cheesecake batter over the crust and bake for 45-50 minutes, or until the center is set.
6. Cool, then refrigerate for at least 4 hours before serving.

Chocolate Yule Log

Ingredients:

- 1 cup all-purpose flour
- 1/4 cup cocoa powder
- 1 tsp baking powder
- 1/2 tsp salt
- 4 large eggs
- 1 cup sugar
- 1 tsp vanilla extract
- 1/2 cup heavy cream
- 1 tbsp powdered sugar
- 1 tsp vanilla extract

Instructions:

1. Preheat the oven to 350°F (175°C). Grease a 10x15-inch jelly roll pan and line with parchment paper.
2. Whisk together flour, cocoa powder, baking powder, and salt.
3. Beat eggs and sugar until light and fluffy. Stir in vanilla extract.
4. Fold in the dry ingredients until combined, then pour the batter into the pan.
5. Bake for 12-15 minutes, or until a toothpick comes out clean. Roll the cake with the parchment paper while it's still warm, and let it cool.
6. For the filling, whip the heavy cream, powdered sugar, and vanilla extract until stiff peaks form.
7. Unroll the cooled cake, spread the whipped cream, and reroll it. Frost with chocolate ganache or powdered sugar.

Roasted Leg of Lamb

Ingredients:

- 5-6 lb leg of lamb, bone-in
- 4 cloves garlic, minced
- 2 tbsp olive oil
- 1 tbsp fresh rosemary, chopped
- 1 tbsp fresh thyme, chopped
- 1 tbsp lemon juice
- Salt and pepper to taste

Instructions:

1. Preheat the oven to 400°F (200°C).
2. Rub the leg of lamb with olive oil, garlic, rosemary, thyme, lemon juice, salt, and pepper.
3. Roast for 20 minutes, then reduce the heat to 350°F (175°C). Roast for another 1.5-2 hours, or until the internal temperature reaches 130°F for medium-rare.
4. Let the lamb rest for 10 minutes before carving.

Maple-Glazed Carrots

Ingredients:

- 1 lb baby carrots
- 2 tbsp butter
- 2 tbsp maple syrup
- 1 tbsp fresh thyme, chopped
- Salt and pepper to taste

Instructions:

1. In a pot, boil carrots in salted water for 8-10 minutes, or until tender.
2. In a skillet, melt butter over medium heat. Stir in maple syrup and thyme.
3. Add the cooked carrots to the skillet and toss to coat in the glaze. Cook for another 2-3 minutes until caramelized.
4. Serve warm.

Roasted Beet Salad with Goat Cheese

Ingredients:

- 4 medium beets, peeled and cut into wedges
- 1 tbsp olive oil
- Salt and pepper to taste
- 4 cups mixed greens (arugula, spinach, etc.)
- 1/2 cup goat cheese, crumbled
- 1/4 cup walnuts, toasted
- 2 tbsp balsamic vinegar
- 1 tbsp honey

Instructions:

1. Preheat the oven to 400°F (200°C). Toss beet wedges with olive oil, salt, and pepper.
2. Arrange beets in a single layer on a baking sheet and roast for 25-30 minutes, or until tender.
3. In a small bowl, whisk together balsamic vinegar and honey.
4. Arrange the roasted beets over the mixed greens. Top with goat cheese, toasted walnuts, and drizzle with the balsamic-honey dressing.
5. Serve immediately.

Fennel and Orange Salad

Ingredients:

- 2 fennel bulbs, thinly sliced
- 2 oranges, peeled and segmented
- 1 tbsp olive oil
- 1 tbsp white wine vinegar
- Salt and pepper to taste
- Fresh dill for garnish

Instructions:

1. In a large bowl, combine fennel slices and orange segments.
2. In a small bowl, whisk together olive oil, white wine vinegar, salt, and pepper.
3. Pour dressing over the fennel and orange mixture and toss to combine.
4. Garnish with fresh dill and serve chilled.

Mulled Wine

Ingredients:

- 1 bottle red wine
- 1/4 cup brandy
- 1 orange, sliced
- 6 whole cloves
- 3 cinnamon sticks
- 1/4 cup honey or sugar (to taste)
- 1 star anise (optional)

Instructions:

1. In a large pot, combine red wine, brandy, orange slices, cloves, cinnamon sticks, and star anise.
2. Heat over medium heat until the wine is warm, then reduce the heat and simmer for 20-30 minutes.
3. Stir in honey or sugar to taste.
4. Strain out the spices and serve warm.

Hot Chocolate Bar

Ingredients:

- 4 cups whole milk
- 1/2 cup heavy cream
- 8 oz semisweet chocolate, chopped
- 1 tsp vanilla extract
- Assorted toppings: marshmallows, whipped cream, chocolate shavings, crushed peppermint, caramel sauce, etc.

Instructions:

1. In a saucepan, heat the milk and heavy cream over medium heat until just simmering.
2. Add chopped chocolate and whisk until smooth.
3. Remove from heat and stir in vanilla extract.
4. Pour into mugs and set up a toppings bar with marshmallows, whipped cream, and other toppings for guests to customize their drinks.

Gingerbread Cookies

Ingredients:

- 3 1/4 cups all-purpose flour
- 1 tsp baking soda
- 1 1/2 tsp ground ginger
- 1 tsp ground cinnamon
- 1/2 tsp ground cloves
- 1/2 tsp salt
- 1 cup unsalted butter, softened
- 1 cup brown sugar
- 1 egg
- 1/2 cup molasses
- 1 tsp vanilla extract

Instructions:

1. Preheat the oven to 350°F (175°C). Line baking sheets with parchment paper.
2. In a bowl, whisk together flour, baking soda, ginger, cinnamon, cloves, and salt.
3. In a separate bowl, cream together butter and brown sugar until light and fluffy. Beat in egg, molasses, and vanilla.
4. Gradually add the dry ingredients to the wet ingredients and mix until combined.
5. Roll dough out on a floured surface to 1/4-inch thickness. Cut out shapes with cookie cutters.
6. Bake for 8-10 minutes, or until the edges are golden. Let cool on a wire rack.

Pomegranate and Feta Salad

Ingredients:

- 4 cups mixed greens (arugula, spinach, or lettuce)
- 1/2 cup pomegranate seeds
- 1/2 cup crumbled feta cheese
- 1/4 cup walnut halves, toasted
- 1/4 cup olive oil
- 2 tbsp red wine vinegar
- 1 tsp honey
- Salt and pepper to taste

Instructions:

1. In a large bowl, combine mixed greens, pomegranate seeds, feta cheese, and toasted walnuts.
2. In a small bowl, whisk together olive oil, red wine vinegar, honey, salt, and pepper.
3. Drizzle dressing over the salad and toss gently to combine.
4. Serve immediately.

Bourbon-Pecan Cake

Ingredients:

- 1 1/2 cups all-purpose flour
- 1 tsp baking powder
- 1/2 tsp baking soda
- 1/4 tsp salt
- 1 cup unsalted butter, softened
- 1 cup brown sugar
- 1/2 cup bourbon
- 4 large eggs
- 1 cup pecans, chopped
- 1/4 cup heavy cream
- 1 tsp vanilla extract

Instructions:

1. Preheat the oven to 350°F (175°C). Grease and flour a bundt pan.
2. In a bowl, whisk together flour, baking powder, baking soda, and salt.
3. In a separate bowl, cream together butter and brown sugar until light and fluffy. Beat in eggs one at a time.
4. Gradually add the dry ingredients, alternating with bourbon, and mix until smooth.
5. Stir in chopped pecans, then pour the batter into the prepared pan.
6. Bake for 45-50 minutes, or until a toothpick inserted into the center comes out clean.
7. Allow to cool before serving.

Cinnamon Rolls

Ingredients:

- 2 1/4 cups all-purpose flour
- 1/4 cup sugar
- 1 package active dry yeast
- 1/2 cup warm milk
- 1/4 cup unsalted butter, softened
- 1/2 tsp salt
- 2 large eggs
- 1/4 cup brown sugar
- 2 tbsp ground cinnamon
- 1/4 cup melted butter

For Frosting:

- 1/2 cup cream cheese, softened
- 1/4 cup unsalted butter, softened
- 1 tsp vanilla extract
- 2 cups powdered sugar

Instructions:

1. In a bowl, combine warm milk and sugar. Sprinkle yeast over the milk and let sit for 5-10 minutes to activate.
2. In a large bowl, mix flour and salt. Add butter, eggs, and the yeast mixture. Knead until smooth.
3. Cover the dough and let rise for 1-2 hours, until doubled in size.
4. Preheat the oven to 350°F (175°C). Roll dough into a rectangle and spread with melted butter, brown sugar, and cinnamon.
5. Roll up the dough and cut into 12 rolls. Place in a greased baking pan and let rise for another 30 minutes.
6. Bake for 20-25 minutes, or until golden brown.
7. For frosting, beat together cream cheese, butter, vanilla, and powdered sugar. Spread over warm rolls.

Spiced Apple Cider

Ingredients:

- 8 cups apple cider
- 4 cinnamon sticks
- 6 whole cloves
- 1 orange, sliced
- 1/4 cup maple syrup (optional)
- Fresh orange slices for garnish

Instructions:

1. In a large pot, combine apple cider, cinnamon sticks, cloves, and orange slices.
2. Heat over medium heat until simmering. Reduce the heat and let simmer for 20-30 minutes.
3. Stir in maple syrup if using, then strain out the spices.
4. Serve hot, garnished with fresh orange slices.

Fig and Prosciutto Salad

Ingredients:

- 8 fresh figs, quartered
- 6 oz prosciutto, thinly sliced
- 4 cups mixed greens (arugula, spinach, etc.)
- 1/4 cup crumbled goat cheese or feta
- 1/4 cup toasted walnuts
- 2 tbsp balsamic glaze or balsamic vinegar
- Olive oil, for drizzling
- Salt and pepper to taste

Instructions:

1. On a serving platter, arrange the mixed greens and top with quartered figs and prosciutto slices.
2. Sprinkle with crumbled goat cheese or feta and toasted walnuts.
3. Drizzle with balsamic glaze and a little olive oil, then season with salt and pepper.
4. Serve immediately as a fresh appetizer or side dish.

Braised Short Ribs

Ingredients:

- 4-6 bone-in beef short ribs
- 2 tbsp olive oil
- Salt and pepper to taste
- 1 onion, chopped
- 2 carrots, chopped
- 2 celery stalks, chopped
- 4 garlic cloves, minced
- 2 cups red wine
- 2 cups beef broth
- 2 tbsp tomato paste
- 1 bay leaf
- 2 sprigs thyme

Instructions:

1. Preheat the oven to 325°F (163°C).
2. Season the short ribs with salt and pepper. In a large Dutch oven, heat olive oil over medium-high heat. Brown the short ribs on all sides, then remove and set aside.
3. In the same pot, sauté onion, carrots, celery, and garlic until softened, about 5 minutes.
4. Stir in the tomato paste and cook for another 2 minutes. Add wine, beef broth, bay leaf, and thyme, scraping up any brown bits from the bottom of the pot.
5. Return the short ribs to the pot, making sure they are mostly submerged in the liquid. Cover and place in the oven to braise for 2 1/2 to 3 hours, until tender.
6. Remove the ribs from the pot and strain the sauce. Serve the ribs with the sauce.

Mincemeat Pie

Ingredients:

- 1 pre-made pie crust
- 2 cups mincemeat filling (store-bought or homemade)
- 1 tbsp brandy (optional)
- 1 tbsp butter, cut into small pieces
- 1 egg, beaten (for egg wash)

Instructions:

1. Preheat the oven to 375°F (190°C).
2. Roll out the pie crust and fit it into a 9-inch pie dish. Fill with mincemeat filling, adding brandy if desired.
3. Dot the filling with butter pieces, then cover with the second pie crust. Crimp the edges and make small slits in the top to allow steam to escape.
4. Brush the top of the crust with the beaten egg.
5. Bake for 45-50 minutes, or until the crust is golden brown. Let cool before serving.

Ratatouille

Ingredients:

- 2 tbsp olive oil
- 1 onion, chopped
- 2 zucchini, sliced
- 1 eggplant, chopped
- 1 bell pepper, chopped
- 4 tomatoes, chopped
- 2 cloves garlic, minced
- 1 tsp dried thyme
- 1 tsp dried basil
- Salt and pepper to taste

Instructions:

1. Heat olive oil in a large skillet over medium heat. Add the onion and sauté until softened, about 5 minutes.
2. Add zucchini, eggplant, bell pepper, and garlic. Cook for another 5 minutes until the vegetables start to soften.
3. Stir in tomatoes, thyme, basil, salt, and pepper. Cover and simmer for 25-30 minutes, stirring occasionally, until vegetables are tender and the flavors are melded.
4. Serve hot as a main or side dish.

Roasted Potatoes with Rosemary

Ingredients:

- 2 lbs baby potatoes, halved or quartered
- 2 tbsp olive oil
- 2 sprigs fresh rosemary, chopped
- 4 garlic cloves, smashed
- Salt and pepper to taste

Instructions:

1. Preheat the oven to 400°F (200°C). Toss the potatoes with olive oil, rosemary, garlic, salt, and pepper.
2. Spread the potatoes in a single layer on a baking sheet. Roast for 25-30 minutes, turning occasionally, until golden and crispy.
3. Serve immediately with a garnish of fresh rosemary.

Trifle with Berries and Custard

Ingredients:

- 1 pound sponge cake or ladyfingers, cut into cubes
- 1 pint strawberries, sliced
- 1 pint blueberries
- 1 pint raspberries
- 2 cups vanilla custard (store-bought or homemade)
- 1 cup heavy cream, whipped
- 2 tbsp sugar
- Fresh mint leaves for garnish

Instructions:

1. In a large trifle dish, layer sponge cake or ladyfingers at the bottom.
2. Top with a layer of vanilla custard, followed by a layer of mixed berries.
3. Repeat the layers, ending with whipped cream on top.
4. Garnish with additional berries and mint leaves.
5. Chill for at least 2 hours before serving to allow the flavors to meld.

Vanilla and Almond Panettone

Ingredients:

- 1 1/2 cups all-purpose flour
- 1/4 cup sugar
- 1 tsp active dry yeast
- 1/2 tsp salt
- 1/2 cup milk, warm
- 1/4 cup unsalted butter, softened
- 2 large eggs
- 1 tsp vanilla extract
- 1 tsp almond extract
- 1/2 cup chopped dried fruit (raisins, currants, etc.)
- 1/2 cup chopped almonds

Instructions:

1. In a bowl, combine flour, sugar, yeast, and salt. Add warm milk, butter, eggs, vanilla, and almond extract. Mix until a dough forms.
2. Knead the dough for 5-7 minutes until smooth. Cover and let rise in a warm place for 1 hour.
3. Punch down the dough and fold in dried fruit and almonds. Shape into a ball and place in a greased panettone mold or a round cake pan.
4. Let the dough rise for another 30 minutes. Preheat the oven to 350°F (175°C).
5. Bake for 30-40 minutes, until golden brown. Let cool before serving.

Chocolate Mint Tart

Ingredients:

- 1 1/2 cups graham cracker crumbs
- 1/4 cup sugar
- 1/2 cup melted butter
- 1 cup heavy cream
- 1 1/2 cups semi-sweet chocolate, chopped
- 1 tsp peppermint extract
- Whipped cream, for garnish

Instructions:

1. Preheat the oven to 350°F (175°C). Mix graham cracker crumbs, sugar, and melted butter until combined. Press into the bottom of a tart pan and bake for 10 minutes. Let cool.
2. Heat the heavy cream in a saucepan over medium heat until simmering. Remove from heat and stir in chopped chocolate until smooth.
3. Stir in peppermint extract, then pour the chocolate mixture into the cooled crust.
4. Refrigerate for at least 2 hours to set. Garnish with whipped cream before serving.

www.ingramcontent.com/pod-product-compliance
Lightning Source LLC
LaVergne TN
LVHW061955070526
838199LV00060B/4123